GENE McCARTHY'S MINNESOTA

Memories of a Native Son

Eugene J. McCarthy

to Annetta —

Eugene J. McCarthy

WINSTON PRESS

Photographs by: Harry D. Ayer, Minnesota Historical Society—pp. 14 and 114; Morton Broffman—back cover; Lee and Palmer, Minnesota Historical Society— p. 130; *Minneapolis Tribune*, Minnesota Historical Society—p. 104; Minnesota Historical Society—front cover and all other photos; William Roleff, Minnesota Historical Society—p. 6; St. John's University, St. Cloud, Minn.—p. 74; Stearns County Historical Society—p. 72.

"Driving Toward Lac Qui Parle River" is reprinted from *Silence in the Snowy Fields*, published by Wesleyan University Press, 1962. Copyright © 1962 by Robert Bly. Reprinted by permission of Robert Bly.

A passage from "The Ax-Helve" is reprinted from *The Poetry of Robert Frost* edited by Edward Connery Lathem. Copyright 1923, © 1969 by Holt, Rinehart and Winston. Copyright 1951 by Robert Frost. Reprinted by permission of Holt, Rinehart and Winston, Publishers.

Illustration on title page: Lisel Salzer

Cover design: Tom Egerman

Library of Congress Catalog Card Number: 82-050290
ISBN (softcover): 0-86683-681-0
ISBN (hardcover): 0-86683-682-9

Printed in the United States of America.

5   4   3   2   1

Winston Press, Inc.
430 Oak Grove
Minneapolis, Minnesota 55403

GENE MᶜCARTHY'S MINNESOTA

DRIVING TOWARD THE LAC QUI PARLE RIVER

I.

I am driving; it is dusk; Minnesota.
The stubble field catches the last growth
    of sun.
The soybeans are breathing on all sides.
Old men are sitting before their houses
    on carseats
In the small towns. I am happy,
The moon rising above the turkey sheds.

II.

The small world of the car
Plunges through the deep fields of the night,
On the road from Willmar to Milan.
This solitude covered with iron
Moves through the fields of night
Penetrated by the noise of crickets.

III.

Nearly to Milan, suddenly a small bridge,
And water kneeling in the moonlight.
In small towns the houses are built right on
    the ground;
The lamplight falls on all fours in the grass.
When I reach the river, the full moon covers it;
A few people are talking low in a boat.

—Robert Bly

Contents

Minnesota Beginnings

BEGINNINGS

Slow, silent, grate and grind of glacial ice
On stone, on clay, ploughing beds for rivers,
Pushing over hills, gouging basins for lakes.
A million years of waiting for the basalt land
With cold winds whining over the ice case
Snow saws cutting ledges and lines.
And then a sound of water dripping,
Telegraphing the imperceptible retreat—
The slow shrinking of the ice shield,
The beginnings of rivers that would flow south.
Of rivers waiting to flow north,
Scant grass among the stones
And sphagnum moss
And that most timid of trees,
The tamarack.

SOUNDS

A bird's cry first,
A weasel's shriek,
Then the guttural otter,
And the snow fox's bark.
Whispers of grass,
The boom of buffalo herds,
The voices of men,
Syllabic, naming the land in simplicity—
Wabasha, Manitoba, Minnehaha, Mankato,
Chipping stones, hard, for flint arrowheads,
Shaping red sandstone, soft, for peace pipes,
And then a new sound: singing,
Hennepin, Frontenac, Duluth, the voyageurs,
Singing to the rhythm of their oars.

WORK

The rattle
Of the yoke against ox horns,
The creak of wood against wood,
Of axle and hub of red-river wagons.
And then the unmistakable sound of horses,
Of harness irons, of bridles,
Of saddles, of leather.
New English names of settlers and soldiers
Of commerce and trade.
Ramsey, Rice, Walker,
And then the many mixed voices and sounds
Of axes and saws and of hammers
Building houses and barns. Germans,
    and Irish,
Swedes, Norwegians, and Danes.

PEOPLE

And later Finns and Icelanders
Italians, Jugoslavs, Poles, and many others
Carpenters, and smiths, farmers.
Ministers, priests, merchants, miners.
Sawmills singing. The hum of the mill
The flutter of mowers,
The beat of the reel of the reaper
The thump of the thresher.
Summer lightning, the line storm.
The drum roll of thunder, the whistle of hail
The snow and the sleet
And the hard-cutting blizzard,
Gunfire in uprisings
The James boys done-in in Northfield.

Family

TWO GRANDFATHERS

One with Irish hands
Playing the fiddle for dances,
Building houses and barns,
Bridges and trestles;
"We will set it and brace it
And I will walk over it
Before it is nailed," he said.
One grandfather with German hands.
A farmer, a miller,
"Set the millstones just right,
Set the wheel to the Crow River flow."
A blacksmith by need, turning iron
Into horseshoes and axes,
Into ploughshares and chains.

TWO GRANDMOTHERS

One lost, never known,
Nine children she bore
And died with the last.
The other I knew—
She crossed the Atlantic at three
And died in protest at ninety-six.
"Death was," she would say,
"Uncalled for."
She could card wool and spin it,
And knit *toe and heel*.
She could cook potatoes
Eight ways at least
And believed any illness would yield
To eucalyptus tea, and brandy.

OLD FATHER

You have turned corners that are
    forever gone;
Born into a wilderness
Of hopes, meager. In a past,
Too long remembered and retold.
Your father, always winning
Old battles in lost wars.
His fiddle always primed for the dance.
You were for work;
Now at ninety-six you say
When asked how your eyesight is:
"Every day is a little darker. But it's not
    so bad.
Most of the people I would like to see
Would not look as good as they did when
    I last saw them.
But I would like to see how the cattle
    are doing."

Birth

You were born in 1875
A year of no particular distinction
Bearing the name of your dead brother
Michael, your father's name.
No complaints: Your younger brother
Jim, you felt sorry for him.
His toy, leg bones and hoof
Of a dead horse.
He made tracks in the snow.
The wind is hard on wrists in the winter.
No one has bridged the gap between
Mitten and sleeve. Wipe your nose
    on sheep's wool
And don't put your tongue on the
    pump handle.
Any time, but especially not in winter.

The Cattle

You would like to see the cattle:
Bring out the cattle, into the yard;
Turn them round and round.
They have wintered well.
The calves are strong,
The cows with calf,
And the old bull
Good for another season.
There is enough good hay left
To see them through a muddy March.
The silage has not soured.
There are oats and barley
In the bins, and one corn crib is half full.
The winter wheat is green beneath the snow.

Horses

"Don't take horses for granted.
A bad collar can ruin a good horse.
Set the bit right in the bridle
and the check rein, the spreaders,
the cross reins, the crouper or britchings.
Be sure that the hames are snug
and the belly-band loose.
The tugs should pull full on the pin,
the neck-yoke hang high and free."
You never believed much in blinders.
"Set the heel chains right
for the fast and the slow.
Give a link for a hundred pounds
and let the evener take over from there."

Horses II

"Never hit a horse in the head
With your bare hand," you admonished,
Rubbing a knuckle of fifty years' pain.
Know a Percheron by the hip
A Belgian by the fullness of chest,
Better as mares than as geldings.
The Clydesdale blaze and white feet.
Never trust a wall-eyed horse
Or a thin-hipped mule, and remember,
A mule can kick with one leg.
A horse, to kick seriously,
Must use two.
Look for Morgan blood, if you want
A horse that's smarter than you.

Cows

Ayreshires are good dairy cows,
But there are too few herds,
The Jerseys too small,
Shorthorns gone to beef.
It's between Guernseys and Holsteins
If your future's in milk.
As for beef
The Hereford is better
For rough grass and hay
Black Angus if you've good fodder and feed.
But good cross breeds
Will do better than pures
If you know what you've got.

Leverage

You knew the measure of leverage
In crowbar, in pulleys
For hay mow and wire.
In eveners and sweeps.
You knew the set of the clevis,
The clamp and the linch pin.
Two horses for rake and mower
Three for the harvester
Two horses will do
For a walking plough
For a riding plough, three,
Two for the plough, one for the rider.
And for the gang plough,
Six, hitched well in tandem.

Wood

I learned from you
The diversity of wood,
Oak and elm
Both red and white.
Basswood and boxelder
Hickory and ash
Ironwood and cherry
Poplar and willow.
Birch, cedar, and pine
For roof-boards and siding,
White elm for well curbing and skids.
Oak posts in dry soil
And cedar in wet.

Tools

Hoe handles are nondescript
rake handles undemanding.
A grub hoe is less than a pick axe
a single bit axe for a master
a double bit for the others
sand shovels allow for some subtlety
but a scoop has no grace
spades are built for legs.
A hay fork has three tines
a straw fork has four
manure forks have seven
a silage fork fourteen at least.
"Wear gloves when you work
and don't strike your nail with a hammer."

More Wood

Hickory for axe handles
Ash for a rake
Cleft oak for barrel staves
Hazel for hoops.
The snath of a scythe must be willow
Both woodpump and coffin
From white elm to stand water.
Broom handles of ash, alder, or birch.
The best firewood—
Oak, hickory, and hard pine
Followed by maple and ash
With basswood and willow
Not worth the cutting
And birch and elm
All right in a pinch.

Nationality

You can tell a German farm
from an Irishman's.
The Germans start with a big barn
and a small house,
The big house comes later.
The Irish start with a large house
and a small barn,
Neither is changed.
Germans build round wood piles
well angled and shaped
Irish wood is scattered and wet.
There are two ways of doing things
the way they are being done
and the way they should be done.

Wisdom

You were tolerant of priests
Doubtful of all politicians
Suspicious of doctors
Slow to take pride
In sons or in daughters
Wary of seed dealers,
Of farm organizers.
"Mark, farmers," you said,
"Who put signs at their gates
Or let people paint ads on their barns."
"Member of Farmers' Organization."
"De Laval Cream Separator Used Here."
"The next sign you'll see here," you said,
"Will be, 'Farm for Sale.'"

Integrity

No one dared
question your word, or
the deal was off.
Now at ninety-five
you don't have much to do,
except one thing.
Wooden churches and courthouses
burned down in the last century.
Birth certificates and baptismal records
gone up in smoke.
Only you remain to say
who lived and who died.
Did Jake Powers live in 1880?
Not unless you liked him, you say.

First Things

Your hands set dynamite
on glacial rocks,
under the stumps of primeval trees.
Held the handles of ploughs,
breaking sod never touched by iron.
Your eye sighted the line
of the first furrow, of the fence line
the set of rafters and roof beam.
You cleared land
drained swamps
uprooted willows
cut thistles and mustard.
You did
what had to be done.

Clothes

You gave up handmade shoes
and tailored suits
with the depression of '29.
Careful now at ninety-five
you ask, "Are there spots on my
tie or vest?" You cannot see.
Dressed every day in the nursing home—
white shirt, tie, shoes, and a suit.
"Always wear gloves
for work and for style."
Do you need a new suit?
It's late in the fall
you'll wait until spring
to see the new styles.

Language

You left good words,
metaphors of horses,
spavined and clever
switchers and cribbers.
You knew cars and their character
Maxwells
Model T's
Stanley Steamers
The Franklin air-cooled
The Reo and Pan
And latter-day
Chevies and Fords
You stayed with horses and cattle.
Each car sale lost you a friend, you said.

Ten Commandments

Don't lend money
To the operator of the threshing machine
To a traveling preacher
To the man who plays fiddle at the dance
To the handler of the stud horse
To the operator of the sorghum still.
Don't trust
The horsetrader who carries
A Bible, along with a bridle
The man who gets up in the morning
Before everyone else
The dog warden
The man who offers to cut your side
    of a hedge
Or one who walks too fast.

A Supplement

Never put a horned steer
In a lot with a bunch of dehorns
Don't buy a horse with four white legs
Unless it's a Clydesdale
If the farmer says his dog is safe
Pick up a stick or a stone
Calf buyers are marginal.
Start pigs fast, in a panic,
Let them slow down to a stop
When you have them
Where you want them.
Start cows slowly, sing to them,
Speed up the drive, near a stampede
When you get them
Where you want them.

Sight

What have I seen with you?
the willows curve
the hawks turn
the burning bush of chokecherries
the naked arch of winter elms
the scale on the wild apple
and the wild cherry, peeling silver—
the fly-wheel's first uncertain turn
the dropping of calves
the turning of sod
the first round of the harvester
the strangeness of shocked grain
the treachery of stubble—
and fire in the bog.

Ending

Now you fold vague sunsets
between the leaves of a book of days.
Each day is a little darker, you say.
You have heard the cries of women
gone mad on the prairie,
being taken away in spring wagons
because, they said, the grass
did not turn green in May.
Nervous horses, husbands uncertain,
going toward the city of the asylums.
It was the spring of no hope
not the winter of despair
that made the difference,
you said.

MOTHER

Of tolerance, of strength, of gentleness
Of quiet voice, certainty, security.
Warming frost-bitten hands between her own.
Uncomplaining over knickers torn
In vaulting fences or leap-frogging
The Post Office water fountain.
Salvaging for supper, from after-school
    attack,
A few fresh-baked biscuits.
Laughing at the skillet as sons engaged
In sly, morning pancake-eating contests.
Letting herself be fooled by obvious tricks.
Asking their help in taking frozen clothes,
Especially an uncle's winter underwear,
    off the line,
And bending, with mad laughter, the frozen
Arms and legs, like brittle bones,
    into the wicker basket.
She knew what made boys happy,
And later, grown sons.

OLDER SISTERS

Sisters will say,
"I'm going to tell mother on you"
But most of the time they won't.

They will scream
"Come home from the park"
Before the game is done
(They are afraid of the dark).

But say to bullying boys
"Leave him alone, he's my brother"
And fluff at them like angry hens

They will chase you off the porch
When they have company
Control the radio and phonograph.

But do surprising things,
Like baking lemon pies
On days when nothing is expected.

MY BROTHER

"You always did it the hard way,
   like your mother,"
your father and mine said.
Fighting bigger boys; crying,
with your eyes shut, but brave.
Our voices sounded in the hollow culverts
as we staggered through, Atlases, holding
the world on our rounded shoulders.
We hung from the apple trees
like apes, or ripe fruit with two stems.
Playing catch for hours in the sun.
For days, for years,
tossing a ball back and forth.
Try your fastball. My brother,
the righthanded pitcher.
Try me, the first baseman,
with a low throw—in the dirt.

MY COUSIN LORRAINE

There were older cousins then.
She was one. Noted as her brother,
Fred, who had driven an ambulance
    in World War I.
People, seeing a cloud of dust behind a car
On the county road, said, "Here comes Fred."
She, the best piano player in the county,
    for sure.
That was the reach of our knowledge, though
Some held there was none better,
    even in Minneapolis.
She played for the silent movies.
Out of the small circle of light
From the gooseneck lamp. There flowed
From her fingers joy and sorrow,
Love and hate, peace and war,
Storms and serenity.
Sometimes she played in the dark.

MY COUSIN LORRAINE II

For thirty years, the anchor of the
   Dixie Five;
Saturday night dances, weddings,
   church bazaars.
Saxophone players came and went, the best—
Candy Werner. And trumpet players, from
Steve Zitlow to Lewis Lundemo, two generations
Spread. My brother on the trombone, and as
A vocalist, much like Rudy Vallee, some said.
He said, "Not so, but unique."
Drummers in succession hired from Litchfield,
The county seat.
Now at eighty-eight
Confined to a Hammond organ.
No jazz piano, no heavy beat, no stride.
"Arthritis," she says with a soft smile.
It's not the same.

Children

THE CLOCK
(To Ellen)

"The clock passes the time—
Doesn't it, my daddy?"
Wisdom of the world asked
in four-year-old brown-eyed
certainty—Time—
encompassing without pause
unmarked duration
continuum without commas.

We strike it to measure,
water drops, sand, notched wheels,
impulses and escaping ions.
No answer yet, my darling.

All come to this knowledge.
You are the only clock,
passing the time.

BICYCLE RIDER
(To Mary)

Teeth bare to the wind
Knuckle-white grip on handle bars
You push the pedals of no return,
Let loose new motion and speed.
The earth turns with the multiplied
Force of your wheels.
Do not look back.
Feet light on the brake
Ride the bicycle of your will
Down the spine of the world,
Ahead of your time, into life.
I will not say—
Go slow.

MARGARET

She is hard to find.
Her eyes are speckled,
Her nose is freckled,
Her hair between chestnut and brown.
(Her smile is almost a frown.)
She lives in a room full of posters
    and pictures
With a brindle dog and a calico cat
And a sand-colored gerbil that is really
    a rat.
If it weren't for the windows and door
You could not tell a wall from the ceiling
    or floor.

She's a trout in the sun,
A fawn in the shade,
A chameleon, changing her color.

Asked to use an umbrella, she will maintain
That she's had little trouble with rain.

MICHAEL

It is good to be careful, and wise:
You came home from your first day
Of preschool religious education
With advice for God.
You would not burn up the earth at the end,
But keep it for a ball to bounce.

Winner of the sculpture contest at
   the gallery.
Toothpicks the material.
What did you have in mind? No principle,
But to "build higher than the next kid."

Sixth-grade ancient history.
What would you have liked to have been
If alive then? The choices:
An emperor, a soldier, a martyr.
"No," you wrote, "a lion."
And after the action,
You said to an old, experienced lion,
"Those were brave people we just ate."
"Yes," he replied, "they were Christians.
They liked to die for their faith."

You conclude. "I wish I were a Christian
So that I could die for my faith.
But I am a lion."

Watkins, Minnesota

OUR DAYS

Our days were yellow and green.
We marked the seasons with respect,
but spring was ours. We were shoots
and sprouts, and greenings.
We heard the first word
that fish were running in the creek.
Secretive, we went with men into sheds
for torches and tridents
for nets and traps.
We shared the wildness of that week,
in men and fish. First fruits
after the winter. Dried meat gone,
the pork barrel holding only brine.
Bank clerks came out in skins,
teachers in loin clouts,
while game wardens drove in darkened cars,
watching the vagrant flares
beside the fish-mad streams, or crouched
at home to see who came and went,
holding their peace,
surprised by violence.

FREEDOM

We were spendthrift of time.
A day was not too much to spend
to find a willow right for a whistle
to blow the greenest sound the world has
    ever heard.
Another day to search the oak and
    hickory thickets,
geometry and experience run together
to choose the fork, fit
for a sling.
Whole days long we pursued the spotted frogs
and dared the curse of newts and toads.
New Adams, unhurried, pure,
    we checked the names
given by the old.
Some things we found well titled:
bloodroot for sight
skunks for smell
crabapple for taste
yarrow for sound
mallow for touch.
Some we found named ill, too little
    or too much
or in a foreign tongue.
These we challenged with new names.

SPACE MEN

Space was our preoccupation,
infinity, not eternity, our concern.
We were strong-bent on counting,
the railroad ties, so many to a mile,
the telephone poles, the cars that passed,
marking our growth against the door frames.

The sky was a kite,
I flew it on a string, winding
it in to see its blue, again
to count the whirling swallows
and read the patterned scroll
    of blackbirds turning,
to check the markings of the hawk,
and then letting it out to the end
of the last pinched inch of
string, in the vise of thumb and finger.

TIME BEGAN

One day the string broke.
The kite fled over the shoulder of the world,
but reluctantly, reaching back in great lunges
as lost kites do, or as a girl running
in a reversed movie, as at each arched step,
    the earth
set free, leaps forward, catching
her farther back,
the treadmill doubly betraying,
remote and more remote.

Now I lie on a west-facing hill in October.
The dragging string having circled the world,
    the universe,
crosses my hand in the grass. I do not
    grasp it.
It brushes my closed eyes. I do not open.
That world is no longer mine, but for
    remembrance.
Space ended then, and time began.

THE WILD HONEY MAN

Charlie Schultz, the wild honey man,
Would come in the fall,
His jars filled with the richness
He had taken from bees
From their hoard places
In hollow trees at the edge of the woods.
Bees that ploughed the clover,
Wrestled and tumbled in flowers,
Laid their harvest, not random in wax,
But in measured hexagonal bins.
He knew what he had
By taste and by smell
"You would like a mild basswood?
The brown taste of buckwheat?
The strange taste of thistle bloom?"
"Here it is!"

THE PUBLIC SCHOOL GROUNDS

The diagonal dark path
ran across the grounds.
False grass beside it grew
and told all that it knew
of everyone who passed,
of every lad and lass
who lay upon it
in the night.

It ran beneath black walnut trees
that each June deceived
with promises of meat
but in the autumn held but dust
in worm-drilled hulls.

Beyond it stood the public school,
sealed summer sepulcher of heresy.
The coal chute beckoned those
who craved to know
how learning lived
behind locked doors
and braved the cellar dark
and creaking stairs to see
pale blackboards, books
lying like poisoned pigeons
on the floor, husks of flies
sucked dry by spiders
and bees with pollen-laden thighs,
their myriad eyes deceived by glass,
dead or dying on windowsills.

Temptation lurked
in outdoor toilets
padlocked to preserve until September
the janitorial purgation
of sandpaper and plane,
leaving pale spots where once
the facts of life
and who loved whom were told.

On still nights, iron swings
clanged in the calm.
Dead children had come back to play,
old women said.

Each boy at twelve was dared
to walk at night the diagonal path,
not break and run.
Each step no faster than the first
to prove, to prove, he could.

LYDIA PINKHAM
(On the Way Home from School)

Mysterious lady of the drugstore window
You with your ruff and your ruffles
Your flowered bonnet, shirtwaist and
    modest bustle.
Your pleated skirt and sun umbrella
Your white stockings and high-buttoned shoes
What is the secret of your compound?
Small boys on the way home from school
Are asking.

BEN KRIPNER, THE BLACKSMITH

Vulcan at your forge.
Muscled bare arms
Gloves and leather apron
You dealt in fire and iron
Ploughshares and chains.
Galaxies spun from your grinding wheel
Comets and shooting stars out of coke
When the bellows stirred.
The scream of metal in tempering water
The smell of burnt bone, there in the gloom
The red-hot shoe on hooves,
Horses, monsters, helpless on three legs
As you held the fourth, quickly snatched
From the floor, there between your knees,
And set the nails and clinched them.

THE STRANGE ONES

There was a place there for strange ones:
Perhaps we shall know them, some day.
One who watched every sunset
For forty years, through a cloud of Corn Cake
Tobacco smoke. He gave small boys the sacks
To hold marbles.
One who in all seasons but winter sat under
A boxelder and moved each day with the sun,
    a dial.
Fritzie Nistle, the master whistler,
who gathered us round him on Saturday nights.
A cross-legged Pan, he sat on an empty
    cream can
outside the produce station and blew tunes
out of his folded hands.
And there were the quiet ones, women
who stayed in houses.

LITANY OF THE SAINTS AND OTHERS

Mathilda Ophoven
Minnie Quast
Lucinda Nistler
Verena Brixius
Anastasia Dockendorf
Lucille Hoeckenpoeller
Mercedes Meierhofer
Leila Kielty
Cleo Klitzke
Eva Werner
Louise Heinricks
Agnes Schoenecker
Miss Vossen, the piano teacher
Mary Eaton, the milliner
Sisters Ancilla, Lucetta, Eucharista,
    St. Helen, and Edicta
Florence
Olga
Evelyn Eklund
Cousins Esther, Rita, and Rose
Evelyn, Margaret, and Ancilla Theis

LITANY OF THE SAINTS AND OTHERS II

Waldo Eklund
Basilius Quast
Alvin Tellers
Ray Stelton
Tony Schommer
Martin Kaufman
Leo and Leander Shreiner
Bill May
Swede Ackerman
Clarence Klein
Oscar Eklund
The Theises, Al, Oscar, and Ewald
Lewis Lundemo and his brother, Victor
Dewey Wortz and Mike, his brother
Dr. Brigham
The Manuels
"Span" nee Andrew
"Stub" nee Aloysius
"Boom" nee Louis
"Putch" nee Ethelene
"Tamp" nee Gertrude
"Pat" nee Edwin
"Dan" for Daniel, and "Billy" for William
"Nups" for Norbert, Ley, Loesch, and Kline
Fr. Roemer
Pep Weber
Polly Turner, the pool shark

MY LIFE IN THE GREAT SOO LEAGUE

From time to time youngsters have asked me what I did for entertainment while growing up in rural Minnesota during the 1920's and 1930's. It is a perfectly reasonable question. Commercial television was non-existent, of course, and few towns had motion-picture theaters. Perhaps a dozen golf courses blanket the area today, but there were not many back then. And while most of the lakes in the Land of 10,000 Lakes had already been formed, motorboating remained something for the future. So the range of activities was limited, and the lack of spending money during the Depression narrowed the range even more.

Fortunately, there were two inexpensive and popular pastimes available on Sunday afternoons in our area. One was listening to Father Coughlin on the radio; the other was watching or playing baseball in the Great Soo League. The only problem came if one happened to like both. Then he had to make a choice, because Father Coughlin came on while the games were being played. For me, however, the choice wasn't very difficult. Father Coughlin, a priest in Detroit, was a radical social and political reformer. He was a kind of socialist when it came to the economy, believing in the distribution of the wealth. His foreign policy was of another order, based to a large extent upon his acceptance of the Protocols of Zion as true.

The Great Soo League, in which I played for five years, belonged to a baseball era that is fast-fading.

It was a time when there were few distractions from the outside world, and all attention focused on the local team. If you were fortunate enough to make the lineup, you possessed an automatic mark of distinction. Or if you were a fan, you went out on Sunday afternoons and rooted for the farmers and blacksmiths and school teachers and students and merchants who represented the community on the ballfield. We took the games seriously, which was part of the fun. And it was a pretty good brand of baseball most of the time.

Although the Great Soo League was typical of the country baseball leagues that existed in Minnesota and other states, I suspect it was a bit more organized and successful than some of its counterparts. It began operation as an eight-team league in the late twenties and lasted nearly forty years. The teams came mostly from the farming areas northwest of Minneapolis-St. Paul. Some towns dropped out along the way, but there were always replacements.

The name of the league was an amalgam of the two east-west railroad lines—the Saulte Sainte Marie (known as the Soo Line) and the Great Northern, which ran parallel to the Soo and about fifteen miles to the north. Originally, half the towns in the league resided along one line and half along the other. A cousin of mine, who was there when the league was founded, has told me there was a great discussion in deciding the league's name. But rational men prevailed, and their final choice was a fine tribute to the art of compromise. Henry Clay would have been proud.

The founders of the league also drew up a strict set of bylaws designed to make the Great Soo truly an amateur league. One of the rules provided that a team could not have a player who lived more than five miles from that town. If a player was fortunate enough to live within five miles of more than one town, he could pick his own team. But if he came from outside the five-mile limit, there was rather serious debate as to whether he was eligible. One year, in fact, the championship was taken away from Eden Valley by invoking a technicality of the rule. It seemed Eden Valley had a catcher named Riley who was working on a farm for the summer. One corner of the farm was within the five-mile limit, but the residence and principal part of the farm was outside it, and so the championship was awarded instead to Albany. But it wasn't the distance so much as the knowledge that Riley was a ringer. If he had been a native son of the farm, he probably would have been allowed in.

The effect of all this was to force teams to develop players from local talent. If your team was short a catcher, you had to search the countryside or try out people in town. If you lost a pitcher for some reason, you had to develop another one; you couldn't just hire one from Minneapolis. There were other leagues, however—leagues not as pure as the Great Soo—who weren't above raiding from afar, and who lured a coveted player with a little money. To counteract this, a slight bending of the Great Soo's amateur rules was permitted. If an outstanding pitcher from, say, my hometown of Watkins had been offered ten or twenty-five dollars a game to pitch for non-league towns like Watertown or Delano, Great Soo officials might say, "Well, under those circumstances . . . ." And then Watkins would be permitted to match the offer. But by and large, things were kept honest and amateur.

One nice thing about the league was that age was no barrier. My brother Austin, a pitcher, made it when he was fourteen. I started when I was sixteen and a freshman in college. I played until I graduated, then came back home for a summer when I was twenty-nine and played another year. I had a pretty good season, but I had lost some of the batting eye that I had had when I was younger. Back then I hit around .380 in my best year.

We had perhaps eight or ten players who turned pro, with a couple getting as high as Double A ball. Our only major-leaguer was George Fisher, who came *down* to the Great Soo, rather than rising from it. He's listed in the *Encyclopedia of Baseball* as "Showboat" Fisher, and it says that he played the outfield in eighty-eight major-league games between 1923 and 1932. I still recall his first time at bat in the Great Soo. My brother threw two fastballs by him and then struck him out with a curve-ball. (Fisher denies this.) That was a good sign that he wasn't going to burn up the Great Soo. But he was still a mean, lefthanded hitter. I was a first baseman and I always gave him a couple of yards when he was batting.

Fisher played for Avon, a town of about four hundred. Richmond was around the same size. My hometown, Watkins, was one of the smaller ones too, at about six hundred. Eden Valley was around the same. Then there was Paynesville down the road, with twelve hundred. Besides similarity of size, Watkins and Eden Valley had something else in common. Both were Irish towns and Catholic, at least Irish enough to have a nice mixture. Paynesville, though, was mainly a Protestant town, and it was considered a major breakthrough when it came up with a pitcher named Father Kunkel, a Catholic priest.

Eden Valley had still another distinguishing characteristic: an unending supply of erratic pitchers. Lefty Arnold was one of them. He'd have great days, and then he'd go wild with his control and just be terrible. Everybody was pretty shy of Lefty Arnold. His favorite pitch was referred to as the "side-hill gouger."

Watkins had a good catcher and a pretty good batter named Pep Weber, whose big reputation was that he wasn't afraid of pitchers. To prove his fearlessness, he'd bat with his head right over the plate. He got a lot of walks that way. He also got hit a lot. But he was proud of his reputation. People would say, "He has such a good eye—he can really lean over that plate and watch the pitcher all the way."

Some of the other towns in the league at one time or another were Cold Spring, Albany, Holdingford, New Munich, Melrose, and Rockville. There also were St. Anthony, St. Martin, St. Joseph, and St. Cloud, which made the Soo sound suspiciously like a church league. But there was no danger of the misconception lingering long if you attended any of the games in the predominantly German towns along the Great Northern. It was there, right in the middle of Prohibition, that one could quench his thirst—if he knew the right place in or behind the stands. The Germans in those towns had never morally accepted Prohibition. So when it came, they made their own beer and developed a reputation for pretty good moonshine. Their most famous product was a corn liquor called Minnesota 13, which was processed from, and named after, a hybrid corn developed at the University. The drinking at the games never presented a problem, however, and in fact it may have attracted some of the better umpires from Minneapolis, who otherwise might have been reluctant to make the trip.

Speaking of umpires, I think one of the things that made the Great Soo unique among amateur leagues was its early use of an organized group of umpires to call the games. The first group was the Northwest Umpires Association and was made up of old ball players, some of them former major-leaguers. They traveled seventy miles or so from the Twin Cities and were paid fifteen or twenty dollars a game. Once the Depression was over, the league was able to afford two umpires a game. This was a definite improvement over the one-umpire days and less dangerous for umpires. It was generally held that an umpire's hearing was more important under these circumstances than was his eyesight. In a game at Avon, with a runner on first, umpire Nelson, working the game by himself, went out to stand behind the pitcher. The next batter came up and hit a ground-ball to third. Naturally Nelson turned to watch the play at first. He never saw it. The third baseman's throw hit him in the back of the head and knocked him out. While he lay unconscious, the runner from first made it around the bases.

There was always great concern about how to score a play like that, or any other controversial play. Should the batter be given a hit? Should he also get a run-batted in? How would it affect the pitcher's earned-run average? Naturally we all cared about the final score, but we also cared about our individual statistics, so the selection of scorekeepers was very important. It was said that the scorer had to have at least two qualifications. It was not enough that he be a cashier at the local bank. But if he were the cashier and was also trusted to clerk a country auction, he qualified; that indicated a sharp eye, nimble mind, and great readiness.

We came up with a fine solution in Watkins. Our scorekeeper was deaf and also unable to speak. His four brothers played on the team, but he himself couldn't play very well, so we made him scorekeeper. After a game, both teams would go down to the local restaurant and check the final box score. If a visiting player started to complain to our scorekeeper, he soon discovered that the young scorer couldn't hear him. If the player still persisted, our scorer would use hand signals to demonstrate how the ball went up, like this, or how it bounced out of a glove, like that. He was like Zacharias in the Bible: "I have written." It was written, and there it is: an error or a hit—forever. He would just wipe them out. Dan Manuel was his name, the best score-keeper anyone ever had.

Despite the fact that many of the country roads in our own area were gravel back in the thirties, traveling in the Great Soo League wasn't especially difficult. We would go in private cars, or sometimes rent a school bus, and the farthest distance anyone had to go was forty miles. If you played a town no more than eight or ten miles away, you would dress at home. But if you had to take the "long" trip, a team with style would rent a couple of rooms at the local hotel and dress there.

It was figured that a team's expenses—bus rental, the hotel, the ballpark, bats and balls, umpires, a policeman to keep law and order, and maybe a pitcher— ran about a hundred dollars a week. At least that was the minimal amount a team tried to make from gate receipts and program ads. At thirty-five cents a head—twenty-five cents for children— and with an average turnout of three to four hundred people, most of the teams achieved their financial goal. Fortunately, we didn't have to worry about buying uniforms. The idea was to get local merchants to pay for them and then try to talk them out of putting their names on the back. The merchants in Watkins, though, wanted the glory— not to mention the free advertising—and so I was the first baseman with "Steman's Cafe" on my back for three or four years. It could have been worse; some players represented the local undertaker.

It would make a quaint touch to say that the fields in the Great Soo were really pastures, but this wasn't quite true. As a boy, I can remember playing ball where the cattle had been put out, but in the Great Soo every town had a ballpark. Of course, the conditions from town to town varied considerably. Richmond was notorious for the sandiest infield. Most of the diamonds had sand infields, because grass was too hard to keep up. But nobody had sand like Richmond, which was located in an old river bed. First base was like a pit, and you felt you needed a shovel rather than a mitt to dig out the ball on a low throw.

In the outfields around the league you sometimes found yourself sinking into a little valley as you chased a flyball, or perhaps catching your spikes in a gopher hole. More serious was the problem of the tall grass that had been cut but not raked. Since a team only played at home once every two weeks, farmers who cut the grass for hay liked to let it keep growing until the Friday before the game. But if it happened to rain on Saturday, or if the farmer was just too lazy to rake it, you would end up playing in deep windrows. I saw a fellow hit a ball to the opposite field one time, and the fielder didn't get a line on it. By the time he got to the general vicinity of the ball, it was temporarily lost in the hay. By the time the fielder actually found it and threw it in, the hitter was on third. Not long afterwards the league decreed that these hits would be ground-rule doubles.

Home runs were hard to come by in the Soo League because few parks had fences. If there was a fence, it was usually in just part of the outfield, and then only because it really belonged to the adjoining pasture or cornfield. The ruling was that you had to run out everything that wasn't hit over a fence, and it seemed to me that those accidental fences were always in right field. It seemed that way, of course, because I was a right-handed pull hitter.

The one time I figured I had an advantage was when we played a park where there was a cemetery out in left field. New Munich had one, and I think St. Martin. The idea was to try to hit the ball among the headstones, figuring that the leftfielder wouldn't chance stepping on his grandfather's grave just to chase a ball. I always aimed for the cemetery when I had the opportunity. In the Great Soo, that was considered place-hitting.

I think it's apparent by now that these games were very serious affairs. Little touches of sportsmanship—such as picking up the catcher's mask after he chased a foul ball—were considered a sign of weakness in the Great Soo. What you did was kick the mask out of the batter's box and let the catcher pick it up himself. On a rainy day, you might catch it on the end of your bat and hold it out to him as he returned from a futile rush to the fences.

The deadly earnestness made the manager's job a difficult one. If a team kept losing, it would change managers just like in the majors. Only the winners stayed on. Joe Meirhofer of Watkins and Mike Ebnet of Albany always seemed to do well, so they rolled along, something like Stengel and Alston. It was a risky office. Ebnet owned a meat market and stood to lose a good portion of his business if he didn't make the right decisions. A manager had to be especially careful, because in the German towns families were large. If a manager benched a member of the family, the whole family just might start shopping elsewhere for their meat. Our manager, Joe Meirhofer, didn't have it as bad. He was in the produce business, and there weren't any ball-playing families in Watkins quite as large as among the Germans. Certain qualities seemed to run in the families. The Glatzmeiers of Albany all seemed to turn out to be infielders. The Ebnets were left-handed pitchers, and so on.

The entire season led up to the playoffs, and at that point the tension mounted to the level of warfare. Even the mere discussion of where the games were to be played had to take place in neutral territory. After that was settled, it wasn't unusual for the two managers to bet each other on the outcome. Wagering took place throughout the season, but those were generally two-dollar or five-dollar bets. The two-out-of-three playoff series was a time for serious betting, and the wagers were up to fifty bucks.

The playoffs also required a little more police protection. In the twenties, when they had home umpires, there were a lot of fights involving both fans and the players. The restraining fences weren't very good, and you could get forty or fifty people on the field pretty fast. There was always a policeman around, threatening to arrest someone, but I don't think it ever happened.

I remember the playoffs with fondness, because Watkins was in a good period when I was playing, and we won the championship four times. We were sort of the Yankees of our time. Our strength was good balance between the pitching and hitting. And it's funny how other teams also took on patterns that seemed to resemble major-league teams. Holdingford was like the Dodgers. It generally had good pitching, but the lineup was full of little guys and they had to get their runs one at a time. And there was St. Joe, who were like Detroit; they would go in streaks—some years good, some years bad. You never knew why. Albany had good hitting.

So that was the Great Soo League: a league with its clowns, its bad guys and good guys, and some who got drunk on Saturday night but who could play ball pretty well on Sunday if you got them sobered up enough. And a league with a great family heritage. When I was campaigning for the Senate in 1964, I'd occasionally be in the Great Soo area and, of course, I'd stop off and see how they were doing. I found some of the sons of men I'd played with who were now on the teams, playing the same position their fathers did.

The league is gone now. Some teams disbanded entirely, while others joined other leagues. The loss of amateur baseball is a serious one. It destroys the basis for realistically comparing your skills with someone else. In the Great Soo, you could say, "Well, gee, I think I can play first base as well as my

cousin. I can play in this league." Compare that with the feeling that a Little Leaguer has, whose only grown-up models are the Carl Yastremszkis and Henry Aarons that he sees on television or at the major-league ballpark. He may be discouraged before he's begun.

Another value of the Great Soo League in particular, and of baseball in general, was the nakedness of each situation. A man was out there in the open, with several hundred eyes upon him. When the time came for him to perform, everyone knew who was responsible. It always seemed to me to be different in football, where a man could fall down in the line and get up with mud all over him and no one except a couple of other players really knew if he had done the job. And it seemed different in basketball too, where just the positive things—the points scored—were recorded in the paper, but never the errors. The baseball books, like bank statements, are always balanced. In the Great Soo League though, as in the major-leagues, it was always an individual and personal thing at the critical moment, and you hate to think that that is gone now.

A COPENHAGEN SNUFF CAN FILLED
WITH DIRT

If things had happened slightly differently one late winter day in 1935, I might well be writing today of how, in a one-on-one situation, I beat the great Frankie Brimsek, who only a few years later was the all-star goaltender ("Mr. Zero") in the National Hockey League and eventually was elected to the Hockey Hall of Fame.

As it happened, however, I was coming in on Brimsek, one on one, having stolen the puck near center ice from the opposition, St. Cloud Teachers' College. Just as I was about to make my shot into the upper righthand corner of the net (I thought Brimsek had waited too long to move out of the goal), I was tripped from behind by a defenseman named DePaul. It was a gentle but dastardly trip. My great opportunity ended in a disappointing slide, along with the puck, into Brimsek. No goal.

If I had beaten Brimsek (we knew then that he was destined for hockey greatness), I would have been able to talk about the shot for the rest of my life. This was my last college hockey game, or at least the last against St. Cloud, and I knew that I would never meet Brimsek in the professional ranks. If I had not beaten Brimsek, so what? Nobody could beat Brimsek.

That tripping penalty led to the only serious fight of my limited hockey career. Actually, it was a series of fights, born of frustration. The first was with

DePaul on the ice, the second with him in the penalty box, and another on the way back to the gymna-
sium after the game. And one more, I was reminded
recently by the man who coached St. Cloud on that
day (Lud Andolsek—more recently a member of the
United States Civil Service Commission), in the gym-
nasium locker room.

Andolsek was a good coach and well qualified to
be a Civil Service Commissioner: he knew how to
recruit talent. After a few years in the nets at St.
Cloud, he became the coach and gathered his team:
Brimsek in the nets; a center named Bjork; a super
wingman, Gasperlin; two DePaul brothers; and a
defenseman called Vandell—all from northern Minnesota, or so it was reported. (Although some of the
names sounded suspiciously Canadian—sometimes
the border between Minnesota and Canada is uncertain, especially in the winter, when the snow is on the
ground and hockey players are involved.) Andolsek
supplemented his core group from the north with a
few central Minnesota players, notably one named
Alexander and another known as "Speed" Winters,
to put together what was probably the best college
team in the United States at the time.

Although the St. John's University team, on
which I played, that year won the championship of
the Minnesota College Conference—a conference
made up largely of church-affiliated schools: Luther-
ans from Augsburg, Gustavus Adolphus, and St.
Olaf; Presbyterians from Macalester; Methodists
from Hamline; and Catholics from St. Thomas, St.
Mary's, and St. John's—we were no match for the St.

Cloud team, which, as I recall, had beaten us 12 to 1 and beat us 6 to 2 in the game in which the infamous tripping incident occurred.

Northern Minnesota towns had indoor hockey rinks in the early thirties, thanks to the wisdom of local municipal authorities, who collected taxes on iron ore and spent at least a part of what was collected in building the rinks.

In central Minnesota we were not so favored. We played our hockey on outdoor rinks, on ponds, on cleared spaces on lakes or rivers, and in all kinds of weather.

My early hockey experience was highly unorganized. There were no youth leagues or high-school teams. There were not even hockey sticks for small boys (at least there were none for sale in small Minnesota towns with populations of less than six hundred). Our favorite stick was a hickory cane, used normally for moving cattle and hogs at the local stockyard. With a little persistence and patience, the local cattle dealers, one of whom was my uncle, could be moved to give a cane to a prospective hockey player. Once the cane was obtained, the critical process of straightening the curved end followed. Hot water and steam, weights and wires were used. The result was not an instrument that permitted much fancy shooting, but it was all right for stick work and for tripping, and excellent for hooking. And it was strong. If no puck was available (often they were lost in the snow beyond the rink and not found again until spring), a Copenhagen snuff can filled with dirt and held together with friction tape would do for an afternoon workout.

We moved very quickly from the straightened-cane and Copenhagen-puck stage to regular sticks, official pucks, nets made by the local blacksmith, and a boarded rink, at the same time progressing from clamp skates to shoe skates and—when one's parents were sure that their children's feet had reached final size—a pair of CCM hockey skates, the mark of hockey maturity. Along with this progress went the acquisition of shin pads, gloves, shoulder pads, and finally, uniforms. It was before the time of helmets and goalie masks, although a goaltender might occasionally wear a baseball catcher's mask. The wearing of caps was frowned upon unless the temperature was getting down close to zero.

Some of the rinks in our area had full boarding. Some were marked by little more than two-by-sixes or two-by-eights to keep the puck in bounds. Some, the most dangerous ones, were boarded to a height of about two feet. Fortunately, there usually was a cushioning pile of snow just outside the boards to absorb the worst of the shock if a player fell or was pushed over the boards.

We were not sticklers for observance of the rules or quality of the ice. We were desperately eager to play, ignoring the temptation of basketball with its warm gymnasiums, cheerleaders, and crowds. Ours was a lonely sport. Age was no barrier. No educational qualifications were required. We played what, for want of a better name, was called "town hockey."

If it snowed the night before a game, the visiting team was expected to arrive early to help clean off the rink. If the ice was bad, the teams might set out together looking for open ice on a nearby lake, usually followed by a truck loaded with two-by-fours or -sixes with which to outline the playing area and keep the puck from escaping to slide half a mile across the open ice of the lake.

The worst rink in the area was at Kingston. The rink was on the Crow River and was maintained, more or less, by the local fire department, which flooded the rink by pumping water out of the river, thus helping to lower the water level of the river and create areas of what was known as "hollow ice," that is, ice not sustained by underlying water.

The Kingston rink was unboarded except at the ends; the willow-lined banks were considered adequate for lateral definition of the playing area. There was one other problem about playing at Kingston. The team insisted on using basketball rules, with a center permanently positioned in front of their opponent's net. We threatened not to play, but eventually, rather than lose a Sunday afternoon's sport, yielded to their rules with an agreement from them that before the next game (to be played in our town), they would study the rules and then abide by them. The game was the thing, and so we played.

Each team had its own ethnic character: the Swedes in Willmar, the Irish in Eden Valley, the Germans from St. Cloud, the Finns of Kingston, and what we called Yankees, persons with names like Eaton and Adkins and Greeley, from Litchfield. The kids from my own town, Watkins, were a mixed lot. Norwegians: Lewis Lundemo and his brother, Victor; Germans: the three Theis brothers (Al, Oscar, and Ewald), Merlin Meirhofer, Butch Leiter, and the goalie, Wilfred Becker; one Yankee: Donald Ehlers; and the Irish: my brother Austin and I.

The game is still the same to me as I watch the professionals play. There is the same stateliness and order of the warm-up, slow circling left and right, the shots on goal, the passing. Then the face-off, the rattle of stick on stick, the ring of skates, the thump of body against body, or of puck or stick on pads. The banging against the boards, the small cries of the players, and under and through it all, the balancing of speed and grace against strength and power, and always an element of surprise, of risk, of danger. Men or boys, it's still the same. The players, skating faster than they can run, propelling the puck faster than they can throw a baseball, defying gravity and friction, test endurance, intelligence, and courage to the limit in desperate drives for the puck or desperate lunges to prevent a score. Then the exultation of a goal, and of victory, with players near exhaustion, muscles aching, lungs burning, and finally the sweat cools against the body, under wool, while the will waits for new strength to undress, to shower, to return to humanity—and the players, like reluctant centaurs having to put off the horse half, become men again.

GIVE ONLY THE HARD, DIFFICULT AND CHANGING
TO THIS PROUD AXE MAN

The first real, professional woodchopper I knew was a man named Jerome Greenwood. He was famous in both the town in which I grew up and in the adjacent countryside. Jerome was never quite a hired man, nor a handy-man. He was a specialist, who did not like either steady or ordinary work. He preferred the hard, the difficult, the dangerous, the changing. He dug wells, particularly when other well-diggers refused or hesitated because of the uncertain soil in which the curbing had to be set. He fixed windmills; he would work as a carpenter, but only until the joists and rafters and the roof beams had been set. He had no interest in putting on roof boards or siding, or in nailing shingles. He was a tiler, a master at stacking grain, and worked closest to the saw in the lumber mill. But all of these good works were fillers, incidental to his real interest and skill.

He really was a woodchopper (not a sawyer or splitter). This was long before the chain saw. His real talent was in cutting down trees, trimming felled trees, and, excepting those cases in which a cross-cut saw was used, cutting trunks into manageable lengths.

Jerome Greenwood would use other men's tools—forks, shovels, or spades—but he would use no axe but his own. He carried it as he moved from job to job, even in the summer when there was little or no wood-chopping to be done. It was a single-bit axe. He carried it either slung over his shoulder or at his side, the head wrapped in canvas or in a gunny sack. He always carried an extra handle. The handles of his axe were what distinguished the tool more than the head. They were longer and thinner than those of the axes of lesser woodchoppers and splitters, and the experts said that the handles, coupled with the length of his arms (he was over six feet four), gave the great speed to the axe head when he chopped.

He carried the extra handle, not because he might have to replace a handle chewed away near the head, as is sometimes the case with careless choppers, nor because it was likely that he might break a handle due to a misdirected blow. He knew that eventually even the best handle, in use by the best chopper, would break from what today is called "material fatigue," first identified in the disintegration of Emerson's famous "One Horse Shay."

In addition to the stand-by handle which he carried with him, he always had two or three handles, or the wood for handles, in various stages of preparation for their ultimate use. These he would leave with friends along his working way.

His knowledge of both the theory of axe handles and of the craft of making handles was comparable to that of great handle makers such as those described by Ray Stannard Baker and Robert Frost. He held, as did Baptiste, the expert of Frost's poem, that the wood must be "good hick'ry, what's grow crooked. De second growt." He believed, as Baker, that one should make no more than one handle out of a single log, which should be cut when at least head high, with no cracks or fissures showing too rapid growth. He may have held, with Jake Sisk of Woodville, that the tree should be cut in December because trees cut in that month, according to Jake, have neither worms nor worm holes. But I never heard Jerome recommend a month for cutting.

After cutting his tree and trimming it down to size, he put it under the rafters of a cow barn for winter drying. A cow barn, he believed, was a very good place, if not the best, for early drying, as it was warm but moist from the breath of the cows and would allow the wood to dry slowly without splitting.

When summer came he followed the Baker rule and moved it to a dry room, preferably the one above farm kitchens where seed corn is kept, and which he accepted had a special kind of drying power. And then in late fall, he took it down to begin the shaping, finishing his work with glass and sandpaper and finally treating the wood with boiled oil when he could bend it like a sword across his knee and sight the slight bow to the left—just right for a lefthanded chopper.

Of Minnesota

EARLY SPRING

Black is the color
of the early spring
Black birds sit bravely
on weak reeds and old
corn stalks and scold
Brown birds hide
in brush and balk
Black cats are bold
Crouched on fenceposts
they balance the world
Calico cats are cowardly
They cringe and crawl in winter grass
Black roosters crow
and take full strides
White roosters mince
and are asthmatic
Black horses prance and stamp
in frozen pastures
Pale horses tremble in the cold
and are arthritic
Black cows come out of barns
wintered well and sleek
Brindle cows are gaunt and weak
Black bulls are brash. They bellow
and rattle barn stalls with knobby heads
Red bulls complain and are phlegmatic

Ploughed lands lie
beside gray stubble, black—
as velvet, threatening
to turn green

RUINS
(And Relics)

Some things will not go away:
Old mills leave stones and wheels
pickle vats resist decay
brewery chimneys
ice-houses and old sawdust
banks that closed in '29
(now used for liquor stores)
schoolhouses left behind by consolidation
bridge piers, country churches
filling stations (out of business)
chicken coops
pig wire, old hay rakes
car seats, mattresses, and lilacs

COUNTRY ROADS

There are country roads of no turning
Pasture roads that end in grass
Public access to Clear Lake
The littered road to the town dump
The ramp to the washed-out bridge
To the pier of the abandoned ferry
Lovers' lane that ends in willows
There are bitter roads
Roads not to be taken
Less chosen than the one
Frost turned from
Less chosen
Than the last exit before
The turnpike

THE TAMARACK

The tamarack tree is the saddest tree of all;
it is the first tree to invade the swamp,
and when it makes the soil dry enough,
the other trees come and kill it.
It is very much abused.
It cannot grow in shade,
is put upon by parasite growths,
witches' broom and the dwarf mistletoe.

HOUSE MOVERS
(Memory of the town of Kimball, where people
seemed not to move, from country to town,
from town to country, without taking their
houses with them)

House movers, among men, are not to be
    trusted.
The house that is moved is never at rest,
Jacked up on girders and rollers,
Pulled down the street, against the wishes
Of trees and telephone wires.

Its new foundations are never right—
Too high or too low.
The trees are all strangers,
Distant and nervous.
They shade the wrong places.
Neighboring houses frown;
Their windows stare at the intruder.
There are blank walls where
There should be windows and doors.

And at the old site—
Houses left behind worry.
Why did it leave without notice?
Did it have something to hide?
Which of us will be next?
Better to have torn it down
Or let it die.

Elm trees, in the yard, lean the wrong way.
The willows hang round the abandoned well.
The sumac decently cover
The wound of the open cellar,
Filled with old mattresses,
Tin cans, and barbed wire.
Lilacs slowly close the unused road.

House movers are not to be blest.

TUMBLEWEED
(Tintah, Minnesota)

The tumbleweed never gets
a decent burial.
Not even in a common grave
with leaves and straw,
never matted down
and turned to mulch.

But driven by the wind,
it moves in uneven starts and stops,
like Indians being driven to
less hospitable ground.
A dried and arid spirit, swirling
with Dante's rejected souls.

The small seeds lost in flight,
abandoned like children of the poor.
(No phoenix here, no new plant
out of the death of old.)
Spread-eagled, at last,
against wire fence,
it slowly turns to dust.

THE DEATH OF THE OLD PLYMOUTH ROCK HEN

It was tragic when her time came
After a lifetime of laying brown eggs
Among the white of leghorns.
Now, unattractive to the rooster,
Laying no more eggs,
Faking it on other hens' nests,
Caught in the act,
Taken to the woodpile
In the winter of execution.

A quick stroke of the axe,
One first and last upward cast
Of eyes that in life
Had looked only down,
Scanning the ground for seeds and worms
And for the shadow of the hawk.
Now those eyes are covered
By yellow lids,
Closing from the bottom up.

Decapitated, she did not act
Like a chicken with its head cut off.
No pirouettes, no somersaults,
No last indignity.
Like an English queen, she died.
On wings that had never known flight
She flew, straight into the woodpile,
And there beat out slow death
While her curdled voice ran out in blood.

A scalding and a plucking of no purpose.
No goose feathers for a comforter.
No duck's down for a pillow.
No quill for a pen.
In the opened body, no entrail message for the
    haurspex.
Not one egg of promise in the oviduct.
In the gray gizzard, no diamond or emerald,
But only half-ground corn,
Sure evidence of unprofitability.

The breast and legs,
The wings and thighs,
The strong heart,
The pope's nose,
Fit only for chicken soup and stew.
And then in March, near winter's end,
When bloodied and feathered wood is used,
The odor of burnt offerings
Above the kitchen stove.

FOUR BAD SIGNS

The first Bad Sign is this:
"Green River Ordinance Enforced Here.
Peddlers Not Allowed."

This is a clean, safe town.
No one can just come round
With ribbons and bright thread
Or new books to be read.
This is an established place.
We have accepted patterns in lace,
And ban itinerant vendors of new forms
    and whirls,
All things that turn the heads of girls.
We are not narrow, but we live with care.

Gypsies, hawkers, and minstrels are right
    for a fair.
But transient peddlers, nuisances, we say
From Green River must be kept away.
Traveling preachers, actors with a play,
Can pass through, but may not stay.
Phoenicians, Jews, men of Venice—
Know that this is the home of Kiwanis.

All you who have been round the world to find
Beauty in small things, read our sign,
And move on.

The second Bad Sign is this:
"Mixed Drinks."

"Mixed Drinks."
What mystery blinks
As in the thin blood of the neon sign
The uncertain hearts of the customers
Are tested there in the window.
Embolism after embolism, repeating—
"Mixed Drinks" between the art movie
And the Reasonable Rates Hotel.
Mixed drinks are class,
Each requires a different glass.
Mixed drink is manhattan red
Between the adult movie and the unmade bed.
Mixed drink is daiquiri green
Between the gospel mission and the sheen
Of hair oil on the rose-planted paper.
Mixed drink is forgiveness
Between the vicarious sin
And the half-empty bottle of gin.
Mixed drink is remembrance
Between unshaded forty-watt bulbs hung
    from the ceiling,
Between the light a man cannot live by
And the better darkness.
"Mixed Drinks" is the sign of contradiction.

The third Bad Sign is this:
"We Serve All Faiths."

We serve all faiths—
We the morticians.
Tobias is out, he has had it.
We do not bury the dead.
Not, He died, was buried,
   and after three days arose.
But, He died, was revived,
   and after three days was buried alive.
This is our scripture.
Do not disturb the established practitioner.
Do not disturb the traditional mortician,
Giving fans to the church for hot days,
Dropping a calendar at the nursing home,
A pamphlet in the hospital waiting room,
An ad in the testimonial brochure
   at the retirement banquet.
Promising the right music,
   the artificial grass.

We bury faith of all kinds.
Foreverness does not come easily.
The rates should be higher.

The fourth Bad Sign is this:
"No Deposit, No Return."

Better be wanted dead or alive
Than be a bottle of "no deposit, no return."

The livery horse required a pledge.
The rental car at least a name.
Return postage is guaranteed
On free seed and third-class mail.

Slave ships captained
By men of God left glass beads
On the golden sand.
Bourbon barrels are reused.
Tin cans and old cars
Crushed into cubes
Sent to Japan.

Now leave her here at the nursing home.
She will have company
And continuous care.
No deposit, no return
On the bottle that once knew wine,
The body that once knew love.

THE MODEL T
(To Robert Frost)

You are a Model T painted black.
The choke wire sticks out of the radiator.
The crank hangs in a sling.
Starting you is not easy.
The spark must be set right,
the magneto coils dry.
Your kick can break a man's arm.
On cold days one may have to jack up
one of your hind wheels
to get you started.

Once started you are dangerous.
You are always slightly in gear.
Your brakes are marginal.
There is risk in riding with you.
Your fuel tank is under the front seat.
You run on gasoline or on kerosene.
Either can explode.

You are not exactly comfortable.
You have leaf springs but no shock absorbers.
Your tires have inner tubes
and are not puncture proof.
You carry no spare tire,
only tire tools and patching.

Because your fuel system depends on gravity,
not on vacuum,
you climb steep hills in reverse.
You provide sure passage in spring mud,
have clearance enough for pasture rocks
and for the center ridge of deep rutted roads.

Your fenders carry small boys.
Your running boards are lined with poets.
You get us there.

THE HERON
(Farm Island Lake)

The heron comes before the light
Has quite distinguished day from night.
Where he stands all things turn gray.
His yellow eye rebukes the sun.
Pricked by his beak, all colors run
Through his one leg into the bay.

All day disdained, the dismal fishes swim
About that one deceiving reed
And flout the warning line
That runs from his sun-moved shadow
To the point of death.

Why does the heron wait,
Alone, controlled, celibate?
Simon Stylites on his rod
Looking for the weakening of God,
The executioner who prays
A day before he slays.
When at last the sun, slanting
Beneath his clouded breast, has changed
All things to gold, delayed,
The answer comes.

The heron strikes and kills his wish
For he eats only golden fish.
And that same fish, mirrored
In the heron's avid eyes,
Sees himself as golden and dies
In that belief. Both fish and bird
By the same sun, at end, betrayed.

THE SOO LINE RIGHT OF WAY

Here you find no counted seeds
Or calculated crops
Only the most wanted weeds
Nettles, great thistles, and burdocks
With exiles and expatriates from pot and box
Gypsy plants, despising rows
Alien corn, unhelped by hoes
Asters, lupine, sumac, and thorn—
Stranger plants, of no fame,
Which country Adams across
The fence, look at
As of forbidden knowledge
And refuse to name.

THE HARVESTERS

Restless in the hay mow
Turning in thoughts of the farmer's
    daughters.
Blinking in the morning motes,
In the light let through the roof
    board holes.
Barefooted still, ankles spotted
    by stubble
Yesterday's barley, better without socks.
But today, you pull on gray socks.
Wheat and oats, with no beards
Will run gold and silver from the hopper.
Running water from the pump on your wrists,
On your hands and arms, on faces.
Pigs will go mad in the new straw
And cows on the way to milking.
Two dollars a day and three meals
And you sleep in the hay.

Minnesota Wisdom, Ways,
Persons, and Politics

GOOD-DADDY HALL*
(Variation on a Poem by Margaret Gibson)

When Good-Daddy Hall left town
     (under judge's orders)
He chewed knapweed
out one corner of his mouth.

He stood tall
at the Trailways depot

right there

with the magazine racks
and the one-eyed rainbow oil stains
ablaze in the butt-end rhetoric
he personally rolled.

He was a politician
He said,
     "Leaving don't hurt."
     "I go on."

He said,
     "There used to be good whiskey, cheap.
     In St. Paul. There used to be gambling.
     Easy."

     "Everything sinks."

He ran on like that, a litany,
a nobility, Dante could envy.

Then he slumped.
The bus was nowhere in sight.

He raised a hand, like gray smoke.

It dropped.
        "Empty roads," he said.

His niece Sybyl from Waterloo, Iowa, said,
        "Pick up your suitcase, Adam."
        "Here comes the bus."

He did.

"Adam," she had said. We thought it was irony.
It was just his name.

*Good-Daddy Hall was a black man who ran a
modest after-hours club for his friends,
comparable to that provided by the Minnesota
Club and the Athletic Club for some other
citizens of St. Paul. In continuous trouble with
the law, Good-Daddy finally accepted exile.

WHERE IS JOE ROLETTE
WHEN WE NEED HIM?

In the year 1857, the year preceding the granting of statehood to Minnesota, the territorial legislature passed a bill that would have moved the capital from St. Paul, the site of the territorial government, to St. Peter. It was known that the Removal Bill would be signed by the territorial governor, who was sympathetic to St. Peter.

Enter Joe Rolette, chairman of the committee on enrolled bills of the territorial legislature. With the Removal Bill in his possession, Joe went into a week of hiding. Some historians say that he hid in the swamp area near St. Paul, now known as Pig's Eye Lake. Others say that he spent the week in more comfortable quarters, playing poker with cronies. In either case, Joe did not turn up with the bill until the end of the term, when it was too late for the governor legally to sign it.

Rolette's portrait is prominently displayed on a wall of the Minnesota Club in St. Paul. St. Peter, as a consolation for having lost the capital, was given the state's first mental institution.

On December 6, 1977, by a vote of 9 to 8, the Senate Judiciary Committee reported to the Senate a joint resolution proposing to abolish the electoral college and to substitute for it the direct popular election of the president and the vice president. The proposed amendment was the product of the Judiciary Committee's Subcommittee on Constitutional

Amendments (now the Subcommittee on the Constitution), which had Senator Birch Bayh as its chairman.

On June 16, 1978, Bayh, supported by a bipartisan group of nine other senators, wrote to the majority leader urging him to schedule the resolution for Senate consideration. The pressing argument made to the majority leader was that the resolution should be considered immediately, as it "may be the only controversial issue to reach the floor this year for which the votes required for cloture are assured well in advance of floor action, and the votes required for passage will be committed before it is taken up." As an additional argument for taking it up, the letter stated that for several years leading polls have registered five-to-one support for the proposed amendment.

These are the pragmatic arguments for immediate action, the weight of which seems to be that, since the resolution *can* be passed, it *should* be passed.

Of all the proposals for amending the Constitution relative to the operation of the electoral college, the proposal for the direct election of the president and vice president is the least desirable. The arguments against the proposed amendment are not procedural, but historical and substantive.

The proponents offer as their most serious argument in support of the amendment that, under the present system, it is possible that the candidate receiving the largest popular vote might not be elected president. Such an occurrence, they say, not only is undemocratic in a quantitative way, but might precipitate a constitutional crisis.

It is true that under the present system the candidate receiving the largest popular vote might not be elected. This is not a surprising observation. It has been recognized as a possibility since the Constitution was adopted. Moreover, it has in fact happened. In the election of 1888, Grover Cleveland lost to Benjamin Harrison, although his popular vote was about one hundred thousand votes higher than that of Harrison. There was no constitutional crisis. (It was a constitutional election.) Moreover, there was no political crisis, or crisis of confidence in the president.

Each time a presidential election is close, as were the elections of 1960, 1968, and 1976, political commentators and columnists and editors and political scientists raise the specter of a constitutional crisis (which is impossible) and of political chaos. There follow the inevitable articles about how a shift of so many votes per district, or per precinct, or per county, would have changed the election and elected the person with the lower popular vote.

The second heavy argument made by the Judiciary Committee for the proposed amendment is that it would strengthen the two-party system. They give no good reason why this system, which has been all but legalized through the passage of the Federal Election Campaign Act, needs additional and constitutional support. Nor do they explain why we need a "two-party system" which in recent elections gave the country the Johnson administration, which continued to escalate a war in the face of evidence of its folly; then gave the country the Nixon administration and Watergate; and most recently offered to the nation the Carter administration, which may have established a 20th-century record for incompetence in office.

If this is the kind of amendment that is produced by a subcommittee on constitutional amendments, the practical conclusion is that the subcommittee, which inevitably has an interest in tampering with the Constitution, should be abolished. Proposals to amend the Constitution, from their inception, should be the responsibility of the full Committee on the Judiciary.

Meanwhile, we can hope for someone like Joe Rolette, who, each time the subcommittee approaches the Constitution, will snatch the document and keep it in hiding until it is safe to bring it out again.

VIRGINIA TECH STUDY CONFIRMS
OLD MINNESOTA TRADITION

It was with great relief that I read on December 23, 1980, a scientific report released from Virginia Tech.

Dr. Alvin Leighton, a poultry science professor at that institution, has discovered what seems to be an important fact about the behavior patterns of chickens and turkeys; namely, that longer wavelengths of light, that is, the red and yellow on the light spectrum, stimulate the eyes of chickens and turkeys, or by passing through the eyes, trigger the hypothalamus, which in turn sends a message to the pituitary glands to release hormones to begin the reproductive cycle.

The scientist has concluded that if the red and yellow wavelengths somehow could be kept from passing through the eyes or reaching them, then the hormones that start the reproductive cycle would not be released. If the reproductive urges are controlled, reduced in strength, or eliminated altogether, the birds, both male and female, will be more docile, less agitated. The hens in contentment will lay more eggs, and both male and female birds, undisturbed by sexual drives, will eat quietly and utilize feed more efficiently, largely because they will spend less time fighting each other—even to the point that the tendency of chickens to peck each other to death may be moderated.

All of these good things, good in the judgment of the scientist (the chickens and roosters, the hens and tom turkeys have not been consulted), could be achieved if the chickens and the turkeys were fitted with contact lenses that would screen out the dangerous rays.

What attracts me to this report is not so much its potential for increasing the production of chicken and turkey meat and of eggs, desirable as these ends may be, but that it gives scientific support to the political application of a method of handling chickens that was used in Minnesota over forty years ago.

This was in the time when nearly every farm had a small flock of chickens. Most eggs were fertilized, chicks were hatched by setting hens, and roosters fought regularly. The serious problem of handling chickens arose during the winter months when, because of zero and sub-zero weather, it was necessary to close the chickens in relatively small coops. In close quarters it was not uncommon for chickens to peck each other to death, as the Virginia Tech scientist notes.

Farmers did the best they could. They thought about the problem and concluded that it was the blood on a chicken accidentally wounded or struck by a chance peck which attracted the flock. They then reasoned that if chickens could not see the blood on the wounded bird they would not peck or pick on it. The next step was to seek out a way of concealing the blood from the cannibalistic flock.

Again the farmers, or at least one of them, thought about the problem and concluded that the thing to do was to paint the windows of the chicken coop red or rose-colored—or better—to install red or rose-colored glass and also to put in rose-tinted light bulbs.

The procedure seemed to work despite the word of scientists of the time that chickens were color blind. It may be that Professor Leighton has found the answer, and, that done for the wrong scientific reason, the painting of the window panes and light bulbs accomplished in a limited way what his contact lenses are designed to do.

Dr. Leighton's findings have political application. They may cause some slight change in the observations long made about one Minnesota politician, which was that "If he were a chicken he would be able to see which members of the flock were bleeding even behind the red or rose-tinted windows and in the muted glow of a pink light bulb."

What he might do, or how his behavior would be affected, if he were fitted with Dr. Leighton's lenses, might be the real test of the Leighton theory.

THE MESS IN WASHINGTON

The General Services Administration has announced that it is taking on the perennial problem of pigeons in Washington. Possibly GSA is moved by an earnest desire to help the president carry out his campaign promise (one that is made by challenging presidential candidates every presidential election year) to clean up the mess in Washington. Or possibly GSA is making a last-ditch attempt to demonstrate that it is a useful agency, in order to escape the Reagan ax, despite its recent record of not being able to perform very satisfactorily its statutory responsibilities of keeping track of typewriters, desks, paper clips, and other office supplies.

GSA's announced program is not one of limited objectives. It does not contemplate the use of halfway measures. It will seek to achieve the total depigeonization of Washington through extermination of what is known as "the Federal Triangle flock." Mere reduction of the number of pigeons in the flock will not satisfy, nor will confinement of the birds to specific areas or buildings.

Traditional devices for frightening pigeons, such as stuffed owls and mechanical snakes, will not be used. Chemicals like Roost-No-More and Avitrol are not scheduled for use, since neither worked well in the past. Roost-No-More was introduced for the Nixon inauguration in 1973. A slimy substance, it was smeared on the trees along the parade route. The slime was supposed to cause the birds to skid off branches along the way, and consequently, in discouragement or frustration, to fly away. But Roost-No-More was not satisfactory. The birds ate the chemical and many ended up (or down) sick or dead. The Washington Humane Society was disturbed.

The threat posed by pigeons to presidential parades, it should be noted, is not as great as it was in earlier times, when the open convertible was used to transport elected presidents and other notable persons down Pennsylvania Avenue. The popular style today is the turret-top limousine, in which the president, or another VIP, exposes only the upper parts of his body, with arms upstretched, looking, depending on his mood, like someone either sinking slowly in quicksand, or arising from the grave in response to Gabriel's horn. In either case, the turret-top considerably reduces the target area for pigeons.

In the summer of 1979 another controlled attack on the pigeons was initiated. A company hired by the government drugged the pigeons, using corn treated with Avitrol. Avitrol was meant to drive the pigeons off by giving them some kind of seizure. It turned out to be lethal, and public protest moved the government to abandon that effort.

Several years ago the Carter administration launched an even more subtle attack on the lives of pigeons in Washington, with the effort to reestablish the peregrine falcon in the skies above the nation's capital. This project was conducted by the Department of Interior, which claimed that pigeon eradication was not its main purpose. Pigeon deaths would be only a "natural fall-out;" the primary purpose was the restoration of the falcon. Nature and ecology would be held responsible for the pigeon deaths. The Humane Society, the conservationists, the friends of endangered and deprived species could have no cause to object. The Interior Department did succeed in hatching four young hawks atop one of the departmental buildings, and hopes ran high that the peregrines would, in accordance with the Scriptures, "increase and multiply." Alas, not so. The young hawks have flown. Of the four that hatched, one is reported to have been found dead in Baltimore after flying into a building, possibly standing where once a tall pine grew. Another died of sickness, or of gunshot, on Long Island. Two are not accounted for.

The GSA evidently has given up on sound as a means of discouraging pigeons and will not expand a system now in place on the White House grounds. President Carter once invited a group of poets to the White House. These sensitive creatures, normally attuned to the sweet notes of the lark, the thrush, the cuckoo, and the mockingbird, were startled to discover the strident recorded sounds of the frightened starling coming from a wired magnolia tree as they waited in line to be received by President Carter.

The GSA spokesman does say that as a back-up measure, the agency may recondition and reactivate the long-abandoned electric wiring systems placed on many government buildings decades ago in a vain attempt to discourage starlings and pigeons from roosting and nesting on the cornices of government. The core of the current GSA plan, however, is a no-nonsense approach. Basically, it entails spreading box traps on roofs throughout the Federal Triangle, and then poisoning the captured birds with chemicals such as carbon monoxide and chloroform.

This project may give the GSA something to do until President Reagan moderates his current adamant stand against redecorated government offices, but it is doomed to failure. Pigeon experts know that pigeons can not be exterminated. At most they can be moved about. The greatest American practitioner of the science of moving pigeons about was one Lewis Neid, of St. Paul. The Neid technique might not work in Washington, but it was perfect for St. Paul. At the height of Neid's career, St. Paul had only three tall buildings: the State Capitol on a hill to the north, the archdiocesan cathedral on a hill to the northwest, and the First National Bank building on what was called the upper levee. Neid hired himself out as pigeon remover to church, state, and commerce, but never to all three simultaneously. In this way, the pigeons always had a safe haven in at least one of the three buildings, while each of the three great estates of St. Paul could feel that they were rid of pigeons most of the time. Possibly a Neid-like program, challenging every pigeon sense, might drive the birds to Crystal City or to Rosslyn, where all buildings are nonhistoric and will long remain so.

The Neid experience and theory is sustained by more scholarly and scientific judgment. Eric Simms, the noted ornithologist, concludes in his book *The Public Life of the Street Pigeon*, published in 1979 and based on a study of the six thousand-year history of pigeons, "Pigeons are dependent upon man, and as long as man is around, the pigeon will be too. While man continues to live in decaying houses and retains his wasteful and idle habits, there will be an attraction in our towns and cities for the pigeon. The only way to control the pigeon is to live in a clean and tidier way."

The street pigeon, Simms says, is not "an endangered species." He might have added: not by nature, or by man, or by the General Services Administration.

THE LINCOLN DUEL
(AND JAMES SHIELDS)

According to William H. Herndon, law partner and biographer of Abraham Lincoln, Lincoln once remarked to him: "If all the good things I have ever done are remembered as long and as well as my scrape with Shields, it is plain, I shall not be forgotten."

The scrape to which Lincoln referred, and which has been all but forgotten, was a near duel with James Shields of Illinois and of other places.

The events leading up to the challenge to a duel occurred in Illinois in 1842. Both Lincoln and Shields were active in the politics of that state— Lincoln as a Whig, Shields as a Democrat. Lincoln was a captain in the Illinois militia, Shields a colonel.

In 1842 Shields was the more prominent of the two politicians. He was the secretary of state of the government of the state of Illinois. Had Lincoln not become president, Shields might well be the more prominent in the record of history, for he was no ordinary person or politician. He was born in Ireland in 1806 and after several stops along the way, settled in Illinois where as a young man he taught school and studied law. In 1835 he was elected to the state legislature, where he became a friend of Stephen A. Douglas. In 1837 he became state auditor.

The sequence of events that led up to the duel arose from an order issued by Auditor Shields during the panic of 1837 when he insisted that Illinois state taxes be paid in specie—gold or silver—and that the state's own paper money not be accepted in payment of taxes or school debts.

The Shields action saved the state's credit, but it opened Shields to attack and to ridicule by his political opponents. Even though Shields' decision was fiscally sound, the reality of a state refusing its own money in payment of debts to the state was certain to draw attention and criticism.

In August of 1842 a series of satirical, insulting letters, all attacking Shields, began to appear in Illinois papers. They were signed by one "Rebecca." There were four "Rebecca" letters in all. Two of the letters were especially abusive, and Abraham Lincoln, at the time of the challenge to the duel, said that he had written one of them.

The letters were written in a dialect, liberally relying on colloquialisms, reason to believe that Lincoln had written them.

Whether Lincoln did in fact write one or all of the letters is open to historical challenge, but he did take responsibility for what was either his own work or possibly that of Mary Todd. In one letter that appeared in the *Sangamo Journal* on September 2, 1842, over the name, "Rebecca," Shields was not only ridiculed, but accused of collusion in a theft of funds (a theft in which he had no part), accused of lying, and called a hypocrite and a "conceited dunce." All of these charges might have been passed over by Shields had not his manners and style been lampooned.

"If I was deaf and blind," one letter stated, of Shields, "I could tell him by the smell," and then Shields was described as "floatin about on the air, without heft or earthly substance, just like a lock of cat-fur, where cats had been fightin. . . ."

And whoever wrote the letter added a ribald comment, saying, "All the galls about town was there, and all the handsome widows, and married women, finickin about trying to look like galls, tied as tight in the middle, and puffed out at both ends like bundles of fodder that hadn't been stacked yet, but wanted stackin pretty bad."

The limited number of scholars who have concerned themselves about the duel and these letters are of the opinion that this last passage was not characteristic of Lincoln, who usually was courteous and gallant toward women, and suggests that someone, possibly Mary Todd or another woman, collaborated with him in writing the letters.

Shields demanded the name of his tormentor from the editor of the *Sangamo Journal*, one Simeon Francis. Francis gave Lincoln's name.

Protecting sources, or concealing the names of pseudonymous contributors, may not have been as strongly established a newspaper principle then as it is now. It is also possible that the editor knew that, when aroused, Shields was a violent man of honor and was reputed to have fought several duels. It is certain that the editor also knew that the county sheriff had demanded of another editor the name of a man who had published offensive remarks about him. When the editor refused, the sheriff had horsewhipped him on the spot. Then the editor's brother had knifed the sheriff, who upon recovery had challenged the editor to a duel that the editor had declined.

After extensive exchanges between the seconds of the two parties, Lincoln and Shields, the time and place for the duel was set: the date, September 22, 1842; the place, within three miles of Alton, Illinois, on the opposite side of the Mississippi River (in Missouri to avoid Illinois law). The spot was chosen by Shields, the weapons by Lincoln, "cavalry broad swords of the largest size, precisely equal in all respects, and such as now used by the cavalry at Jacksonville." The layout, determined by Lincoln, was "a plank ten feet long, and fron nine to twelve inches broad to be firmly fixed on edge, on the ground, as the line between us which neither is to pass his foot over upon forfeit of his life. Next a line drawn on the ground on either side of said plank and parallel with it, each at the distance of the whole length of the sword and three feet additional from the plank; and the passing of his own such line by either party during the fight shall be deemed a surrender of the contest."

Just how the duel was resolved is not clearly recorded. It was obvious from the limits of the dueling field that Lincoln being over six feet four in height and with very long arms could stand behind the plank or log barrier and still reach Shields with his sword if Shields came within range, whereas Shields, of short stature, even though he advanced to the limits of the field allowed him, could not reach his adversary.

By one account, Shields, seeing how he had been outdone by Lincoln, burst out laughing. The two men seem to have become friends again, for on the way back from the scene of the aborted duel, one eyewitness said, "In the Telegraph of the fifth, taken from the *St. Charles Monitor*, I notice an account of a historic spot on the island on which Abraham Lincoln and General Shields met to fight a duel." This will be astonishing news to former historians. "They did not meet on any island, but in Missouri, close to the bank of the river, near a 'clearing' belonging to the Mahon family. I was there and saw everything that took place, which was not much. We all returned on Chapman's ferry boat. On the way across the river Jake Smith, then city marshal, about the height and shape of Lincoln, was laid on a bench on the bow of the boat. Three or four with their coats off were fanning him with their hats. I stood near Lincoln and Shields, who were talking. They had become quite friendly again. The latter remarked to Lincoln, 'As that fellow on the bench is about your size, they will think it is you.' I did not hear Lincoln's reply. By that time it had been noised about the city that a duel had been fought and by that time a crowd of several hundred had gathered on the levee to learn the result. The boat landed directly in front of the warehouse where Lovejoy was killed. As she touched the bank 'Jake' jumped to his feet and gave a loud laugh. The crowd saw that they had been sold and joined in heartily and left in disgust. The Springfield party and some others hurried to Charlie Uber's saloon and amidst general rejoicing soon consumed what champagne he had on hand, a fit ending to such a farce."

A lawyer, and friend of Lincoln, quotes Lincoln as saying of the duel: "I did not want to kill Shields, and felt sure I could disarm him, having had about a month to learn the broad sword exercise, and furthermore I did not want the fellow to kill me, which I rather think he would have done if we had selected pistols."

Lincoln went on to the presidency. Shields became a justice of the Illinois Supreme Court, governor of the Oregon Territory, brevet major in the Mexican War, brigadier general in the Civil War, U.S. senator from Illinois, U.S. senator from Missouri, and U.S. senator from Minnesota.

MEMORIES OF HUBERT
A Politician Too Good to Be Vice President

The last time I saw Hubert Humphrey was at the Washington Hilton Hotel at the fundraising banquet for the Hubert Humphrey Institute of Public Affairs at the University of Minnesota. He was being escorted back to his table by President Carter, after speaking to the audience of his optimism and continuing belief in democracy and in America.

We embraced, spoke each other's name—that was all. I had seen and talked to him about six weeks earlier in the Democratic cloakroom of the Senate building, during the time when he was strong enough to return to the Senate. We had a brief conversation, cut short by a senator who interrupted us to speak to Senator Humphrey about Senate matters. At the time of the interruption, Senator Humphrey was reminiscing about former days on the campaign trail and in the Senate. He had said that he would like one more good meeting in Minnesota like those we had known. "You," he said to me, "could give the philosophy and some jokes—I could give the issues and the pep talk. The guest speaker would not even want to come on, and everyone there would be happy."

Hubert Humphrey had a sense of mission, almost a vocation, to spend his life in politics. To be effective politically, he believed, one had to be in office, and to be most effective, one had to be in the most important office, the most powerful one, the presidency. He did not spurn lesser offices. After his vice presidency and his 1968 presidential bid, he returned to the Senate. If that opportunity had not been present, he would have been willing, even eager, I believe, to hold a lesser office, perhaps even to become mayor of Minneapolis again.

Hubert Humphrey was forgiving to a fault. At the 1956 Democratic Convention, one of his old political companions and supporters endorsed Estes Kefauver over Humphrey for the vice-presidential nomination. Senator Humphrey was deeply hurt and distressed by this action of a man whom he considered both a friend and a political ally. At the time I said to him, "I don't care if you are angry at him or not. But why don't you at least pretend for a while that you are? And the next time he calls you to address his organization, suggest that he get Estes to entertain the troops." He didn't take my advice. So, too, in 1964, he need not have allowed President Johnson to play vice-presidential games with him, for he had the support of the labor movement, the farm groups, and the liberals. President Johnson should have thanked Hubert Humphrey for accepting the nomination; instead it was Senator Humphrey in Atlantic City, thanking President Johnson "for his faith and confidence in me."

He and others joked about his long speeches. He did give long speeches—I heard many of them. It was not that he liked giving long speeches and not just that he had a lot to say, although this did figure in the length. It was something more basic. Hubert liked words and language. In a speech, he was sometimes like a trumpet player. He would go along rather quietly with little inspiration, and then the inspiration would come. What he said or how he said it would sometimes surprise even Hubert.

I recall one such experience in the early fifties, during the Eisenhower administration. Senator Humphrey was being very restrained, in language and political deportment. He was being most considerate of the president and of the Republicans. (The press had begun to write of the "New Humphrey.") And then, in the middle of a structured and contained speech, he took off. "Ike," he said, was "a bird in the gilded cage—kept by the Republicans in the parlor, where he sang sweet songs to all who passed the window, while back in the kitchen the Republican blackbirds were eating up the public pie." The speech went on from that to even greater heights. Subsequently, I asked him what had happened to the "New Humphrey." He laughed, and said something like, "How about that? I just heard the whistle blow."

In a way, his gift of language was a political handicap. In American politics you can say rather extreme, even radical, things if you say them in such a way that people don't remember what you said or that you said them. In Hubert's case, what was said was remembered. It was also remembered that Hubert had said it.

Sticking with adjectives and an occasional adverb as a mark of one's language is much safer for a politician than to go with statements such as, "The time has arrived for the Democratic party to get out of the shadow of states' rights and walk forthrightly into the bright sunshine of human rights." Metaphors are dangerous.

Hubert liked what he had and what he was doing. His affection for his family is well known. He spoke glowingly of his father and of the family drugstore, to the point that one sensed that he came close to envy of his brother Ralph, back home in Huron, dispensing pills, encouragement, politics, and philosophy. Being a druggist, he thought, was good work, and Huron, a good town.

He loved his home on Lake Waverly in Minnesota. Lake Waverly is a very minor lake named after the town (contrary to the usual practice of naming the town after the lake). This lake was less than the town, but he loved it. He saw the best in it and talked only about that. It had water. It would float a boat. It froze over in winter. One could skate on it, and it did have some fish. What more can one expect from a lake?

Hubert was loyal to his friends—to those who helped him, and those who hurt him. When he was sworn in as vice president, the person who held the Bible for him was not a distinguished judge or a clergyman or politician, but his most loyal friend and supporter, all but anonymous, Freddie Gates.

Of all the members of the Senate, I think he liked and admired Wayne Morse the most. Even when in disagreement, he would refer affectionately to him as, "Old Wayne, isn't he something."

Despite the standard talk beforehand of giving "new meaning" and "added responsibility" to the office, holding the vice presidency removed him from real and effective political activity, denied him political independence, and left him as a candidate subject to presidential influence. None of this would have happened had he not been vice president, or had there been no vice presidency.

If Congress wishes to establish a political memorial for Hubert Humphrey, rather than passing the Humphrey-Hawkins Act or naming a building after him, it should move to pass a constitutional amendment eliminating the office of vice president.

GROUND FOG AND NIGHT
(In a Small Plane over Redwood Falls)

A cloud is subtly woven over the field.
Day and night together beget the cataract film.
It holds, while the earth, with its burden
Of brush and of trees,
Of houses and steeples, sinks slowly.

Day songs die and night birds' songs
Are dampened by the fog.
Crescendos of cicadas cross
The prairies of the night
And then are gone in silence like the bison.
Ruminant stomachs yield their cuds
And tree frogs
Fall into green sleep.
Spiders lying upside down
Like Michelangelo on his back
Make a ceiling between themselves and God.
Plants rid themselves of death
Spawned in them by the sun.
Burrowing beasts live on as before.
Shrews and moles shelter
In their dark world the hoard
Stolen from the night.

Now owl and vermin do contest.
No winners from the day.
Men in air-conditioned rooms set clocks
Against the night and wait for dawn.
No sign of God is left above the fog.
Only the red-eyed tower stands
To tell of life
Below.